CHRISTIAN SYMBOLS DECODED

Written & Illustrated by
Dan Peeler and Charlie Rose

Peeler·Rose Media

Published in the U. S. by Peeler-Rose Media
a division of Peeler-Rose Productions LLC

Text copyright © 2013 Dan Peeler, Charlie Rose
Illustrations by Charlie Rose, Dan Peeler copyright © 2013 Peeler-Rose Media
a division of Peeler-Rose Productions LLC
8626 Aldwick Drive
Dallas, Texas 75238
CharlieCRose@gmail.com

ISBN 978-1-48496-297-8

Library of Congress Cataloging-in-Publication Data Peeler, Daniel; Rose Charles
Christian Symbols Decoded
by Dan Peeler, Charlie Rose

Summary:
Christian Symbols have been with us since the beginning. Today, decoding ancient
symbols is essential when considering so many of the pictorial representations
artists and writers have created throughout the centuries in their quest to be closer
to God. This book takes us back to their beginnings and gives us the opportunity to
explore the wonders of their world in relevance to our own.

Peeler·Rose Media

CONTENTS

Symbols of
God The Creator

ALPHA & OMEGA

The first and last letters of the Greek alphabet. "I am the Alpha and the Omega," says the Lord God, who is and who was and who is to come, the Almighty. Revelation 1.8

THE CIRCLE

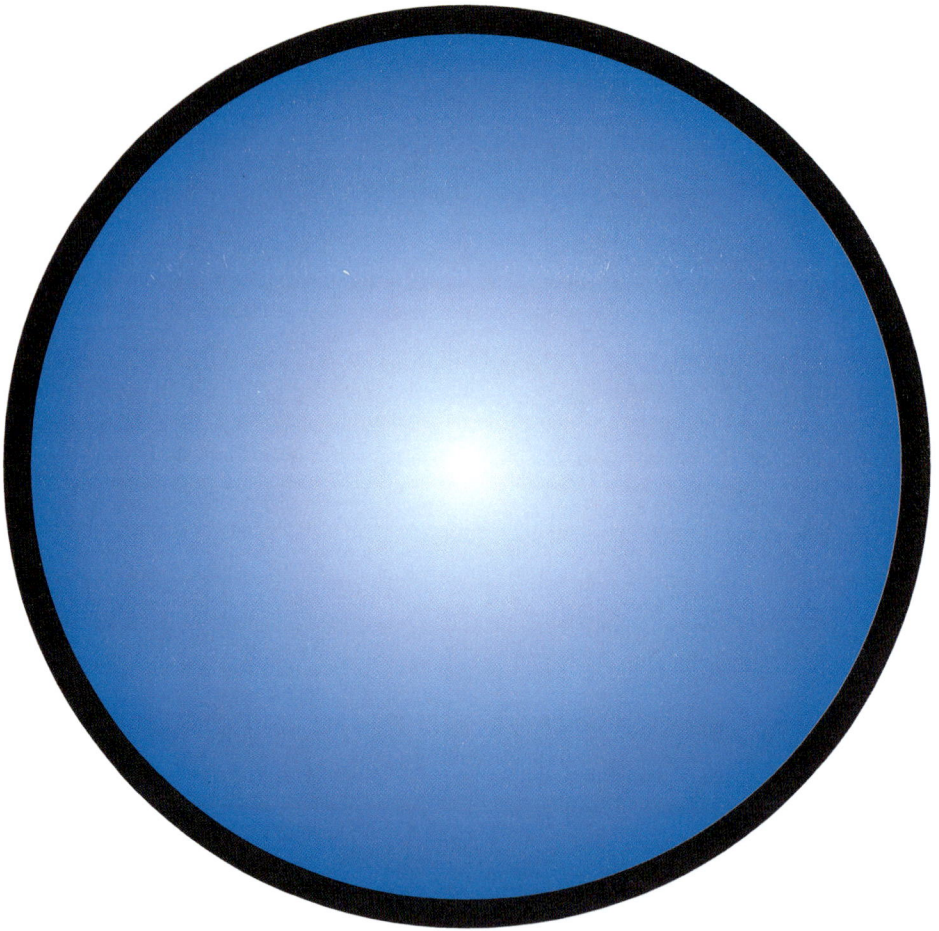

The circle leads back into itself and is a symbol of perfection, unity, and the absolute. It is a symbol of eternity, with no beginning and no ending; the eternal attribute of God.

THE ARK
OF THE COVENANT

Topped with the watchful Cherubim, the gold-plated acacia wood box was the container for the tablets of the Commandments and symbolized the very presence of God veiled in the Holy of Holies in the Tabernacle.

THE THRONE

An important symbol in both Testaments, the throne is a symbol of Yahweh's rule over all of Creation, and a reminder of God's power to judge. The Christian church adapted the throne as a cathedra, a chair with an arched back where highest church officials sat.

Symbols of The Trinity & The Holy Spirit

THE CIRCLE OF
THE SEVEN DOVES

The circle of seven doves around the center cross are reminders of the seven gifts of the Holy Spirit: wisdom, understanding, counsel, courage, knowledge, faithfulness and respect for God.

THE FLAMES

Fire is a symbol in both Testaments of the presence of God; in Moses' first encounter with God in the Burning Bush, in the Pillar of Fire in the wilderness and in the Tongues of Fire of the Holy Spirit at Pentecost.

THREE FISH
IN A CIRCLE

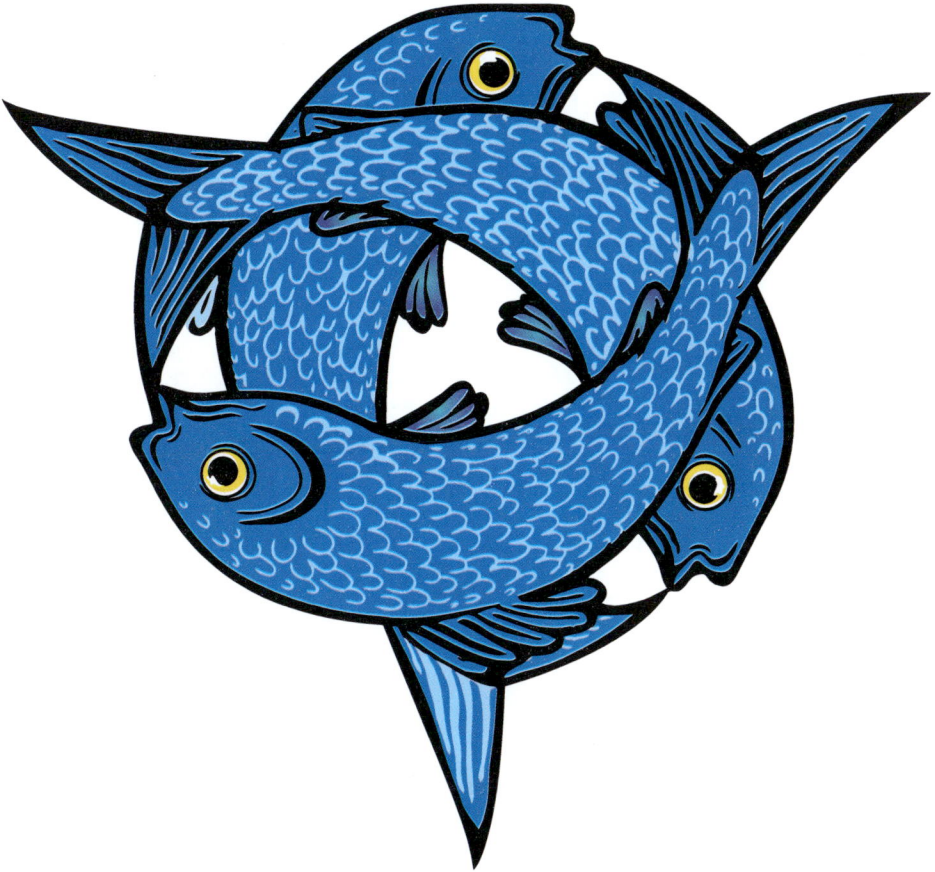

The fish (ichthus) was the earliest Christian symbol for Jesus, here seen as an equal member of the Eternal Trinity. Baptized Christians also saw themselves as fish, born to a new life in the waters.

THE TRIQUETRA

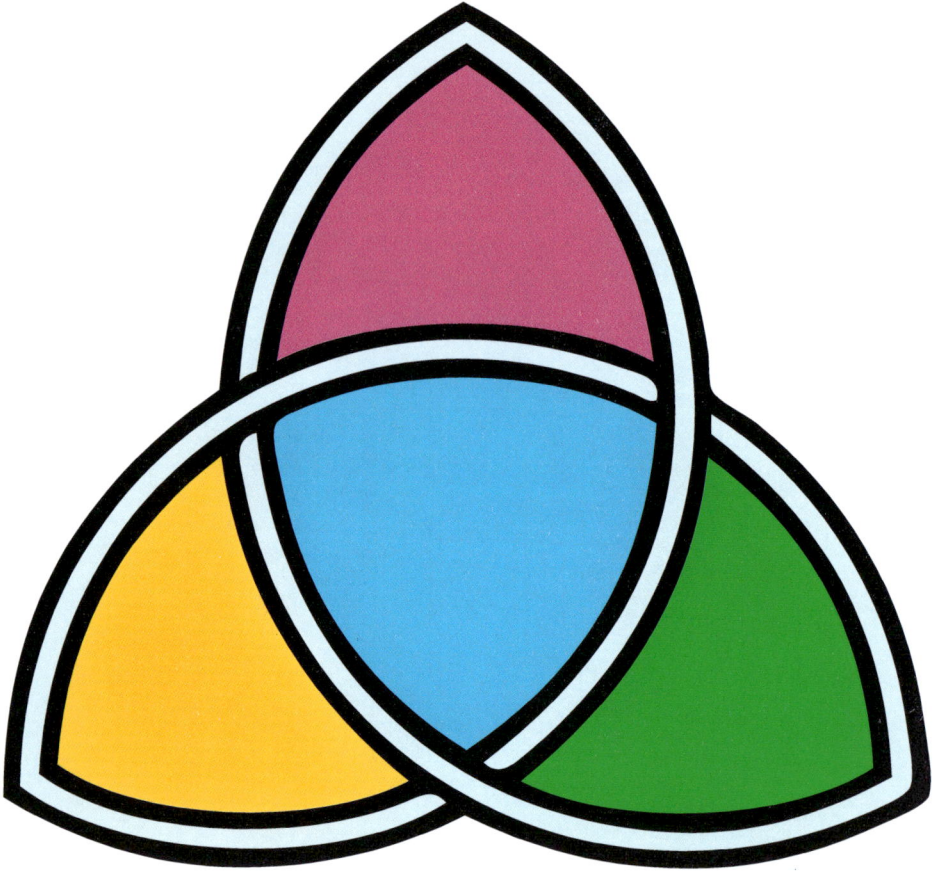

The Triquetra is an ancient symbol found on Germanic rune coins and in the Book of Kells. As a Christian symbol, it is the Holy Trinity with its separate but equal eternally interlocking arcs that have no beginning or end. The center of the design forms the triangle, another symbol of the Trinity.

THE SEA SHELL
WITH THREE DROPS

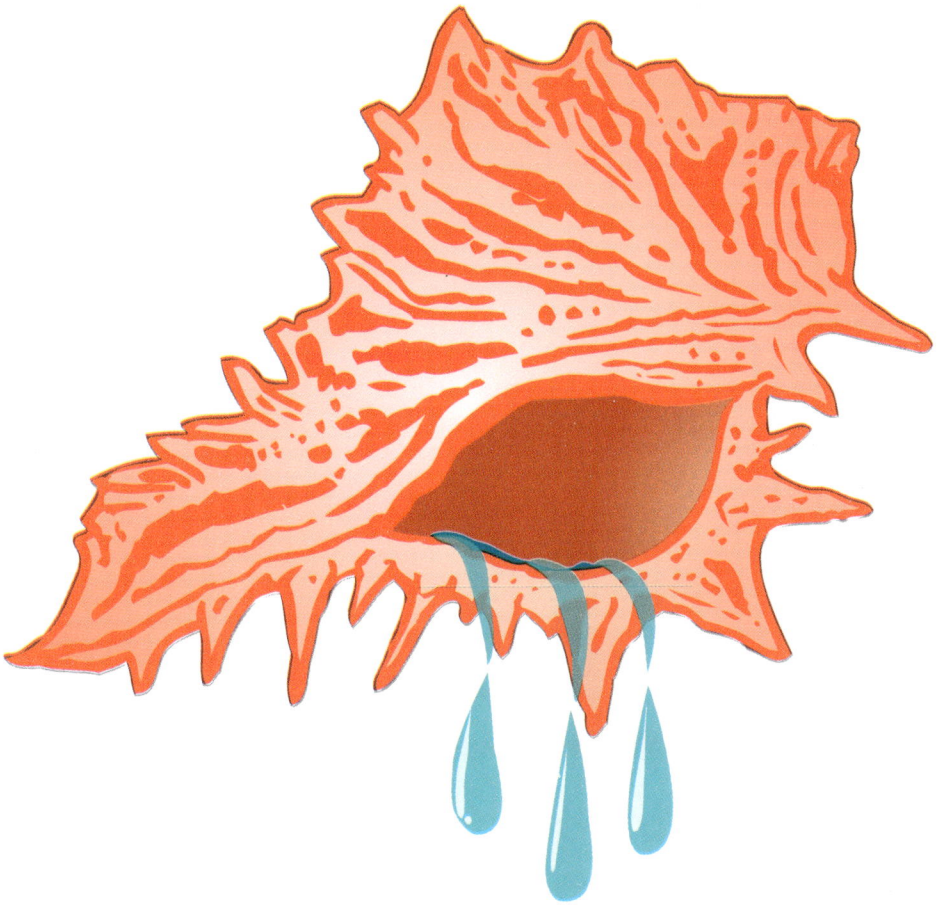

Symbol of the Sacrament of Baptism; each water drop representing a member of the Trinity: Creator, Christ and Holy Spirit.

THE TREFOIL

The Trefoil is a design in Gothic architecture often seen in the arches of window lights, tracery, wall panels, etc. The three-lobed leaf formed by overlapping circles is a symbol of the Trinity.

THE PANSY

Because of its three most prominent petals and the frequent presence of three colors in the pansy, it is another symbol of the Trinity: Creator, Christ and Holy Spirit. The small plant is also a symbol of Christ's humility and is said to have been the favorite flower of St. Valentine.

THE SHAMROCK

St. Patrick, legend tells us, used the shamrock to teach an important lesson about the Trinity. He said that just as the three leaves of the shamrock are equal parts that add up to one plant, they can remind us of the Creator, Christ and Holy Spirit that add up to one God.

THE TRINITY EGG

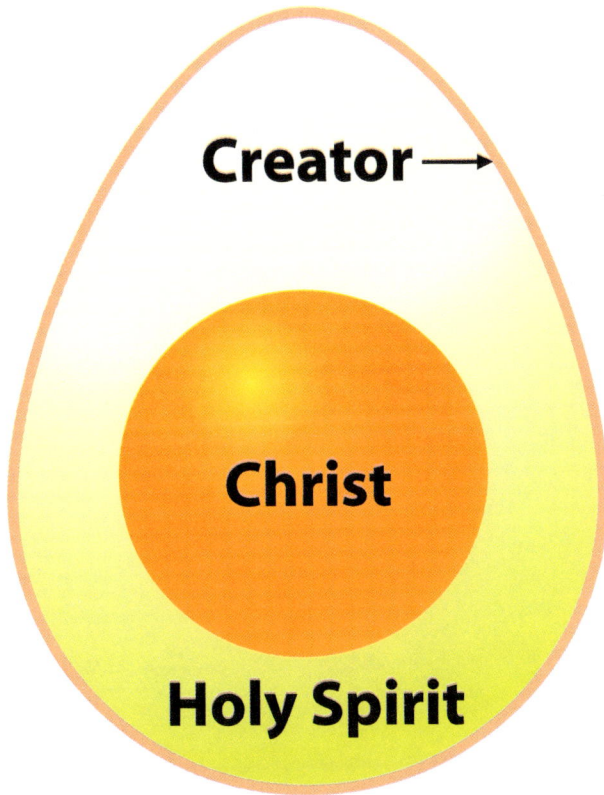

The doctrine of the Trinity can be taught with an egg which has a protective shell on the outside that represents the creator. The center of the egg, the yolk, reminds us of the Christ, who is the center of our Christian faith and the clear, free-flowing egg white, represents the Holy Spirit.

Symbols of
The Christ

THE SHEPHERD

The earliest pictorial representation of Jesus in the catacombs: Jesus as the "Good Shepherd" is both a symbol of the One who cares for the flock and is himself the "Lamb of God" announced by John the Baptist.

THE ICTHUS (FISH)

Probably the earliest of all Christian Symbols, the fish (ICHTHUS in Greek) was an acrostic for "Jesus Christ, Son of God, Savior. It was a secret symbol in the dangerous early days of the faith. One follower of the Way would draw the top arch of the fish in the sand or dirt and another follower would know the signal and complete the bottom half.

THE UNICORN

This mythical animal was apparently thought to be real by some of the ancient scripture writers. (The Unicorn is mentioned nine times in the King James translation.) The pure white Unicorn is a Christian symbol of Christ's strength and purity.

THE GRAY HERON

Because of its ash gray color, the large bird became an early symbol of penance. It was a Christ symbol since it was a destroyer of serpents. Legends also taught it was the only bird that shed tears, so the heron became a reminder of Christ on the Mount of Olives.

THE CHI RHO

A monogram of the first two letters of the Greek word for Christ. Chi (X) and Rho (P). Legend tells of the Roman Emperor Constantine becoming a Christian after seeing a vision of the Chi Rho above a bridge where he won a great victory.

Herald Angel

An angel floating in space, right hand raised in greeting is a symbol of the announcement of the Nativity of Jesus. "…Fear not. I bring you good news of great joy…" Luke 2.10

THE GRIFFIN

An animal of ancient myth adapted by the medieval Christians as a symbol of the dual nature of Christ. (the earthbound lion: the human nature, and the flying eagle: the divine nature.)

TWO LIGHTED CANDLES

Two lighted candles are the symbols of the mystery of the human and divine natures of Jesus, defined by the early church as wholly God and wholly Human. They suggest the Lord's words, "I am the light of the world." John 8.12

THE MOTHER HEN

The hen and her chicks are the classic symbols of a mother's care and protection of her young. Jesus compared his compassion for Jerusalem to a mother hen's desire to spread her wings of protection over her children.

THE RAINBOW

The three-colored rainbow is the symbol of the nature and works of Christ: the blue being Christ's heavenly origin, the red, Christ's human life and Passion, and the green, the new world born again out of Christ's life and works.

THE LIGHTHOUSE

The lighthouse is a symbol for the light of the world. It is a reminder of the teachings of Jesus, who awakens, leads and guides the soul on its journey toward true faith and clear understanding.

THE OSTRICH

Since the ostrich does not sit on its egg, but patiently watches it until the sun hatches it; the bird became a symbol for meditation. Using the same logic, it also became a symbol for Christ who always waited patiently before God, even for his own resurrection.

THE ANCHOR

A symbol of hope; the only source of remaining stable during a storm at sea. The anchor with the horizontal bar near the top was used by the early Christians as a secret sign of the cross and as a reminder that Christ is our hope and the anchor of our faith.

SYMBOLS OF THE RESURRECTION

THE BUTTERFLY

The butterfly is one of many symbols of new life and resurrection. As the caterpillar enters the chrysalis, it remains dormant, and then is transformed with a new body, just as Christ entered and emerged from the tomb.

THE PEACOCK

The peacock loses its beautiful tail feathers yearly, but grows new ones, which remind us of the new life of resurrection. In the middle ages, the bird's spectacular iridescent colors also served as symbols of the joys of the afterlife.

THE TREE CROSS

The Tree Cross is a type of cross with branches, leaves and fruit growing out of it, symbolizing the restoration of the Tree of Life from the Garden of Eden story. The vital and fruitful cross shows the victory of life over death.

THE STAG

The majestic animal became popular on coats of arms in the middle ages, the shape of its antlers being a symbol of the Tree of Life. The animal was also a Christ symbol since it was known as the traditional enemy of the serpent and because its shedding and growing new antlers each year recalled the Resurrection.

amazon.com

www.amazon.com/ your-account

For detailed information about this and other orders, please visit Your Account. You can also print invoices, change your e-mail address and payment settings, alter your communication preferences, and much more - 24 hours a day - at http://www.amazon.com/your-account.

Item Price	Total
$17.99	$17.99
$16.74	$16.74
	$34.73
	$2.86
	$37.59
	$37.59
	$0.00

Returns Are Easy!

Most items can be refunded, exchanged, or replaced when returned in original and unopened condition. Visit http://www.amazon.com/returns to start your return, or http://www.amazon.com/help for more information on return policies.

Pack Type : A0

amazon.com

DRJV3vmSN/-2 of 2-/
second/7873941 UPS-LEXKY-3DAY

Your order of June 27, 2013 (Order ID 105-4672016-4611406)

Qty.	Item
1	**Adam's Lament** Arvo Part --- Audio CD **(** ** F-12 **)** B008U0FI7M 028947648253
1	**Christian Symbols: Decoded** Peeler, Mr. Dan --- Paperback **(** ** F-12 **)** 1484962974

Subtotal
Tax Collected
Order Total
Paid via credit/
Balance due

This shipment completes your order.

Have feedback on how we packaged your order? Tell us at www.amazon.com/pack

THE DOLPHIN

This intelligent and friendly animal was an important symbol of redemption in the myths of many cultures that lived by the sea. The dolphin was believed to carry the souls of the dead to their final rest. Early Christians adopted it as a symbol of Christ's redemptive work.

THE LIZARD

Because of its attraction to the sun, the lizard became a symbol of those who seek new life through the Light of Christ. The animal also was an important symbol of resurrection because of its yearly molting of an old skin to be born to a new one.

THE PHOENIX

The early Christians used the ancient story of the Phoenix as a symbol of the new birth of the resurrection. The mythical bird that burst into flame at its own death, but rose again out of its own ashes, had always been a symbol of victory over death.

THE WHEAT

The wheat symbolizes the bread of life (Mark 14.22) a reminder of the Sacrament of Holy Communion. A grain of wheat also was a reminder of the resurrection, being planted in the earth and raised to a new life.

Symbols of the Faithful

THE QUATREFOIL

A four-petal flower or clover shape often used in architecture as decorations or windows; a symbol of the equal importance of the Four Gospels: Matthew, Mark, Luke and John.

THE WINGED HUMAN
WITH A BOOK

The Winged Human with a book is the symbol of the Gospel of Matthew, which begins with the genealogy of Jesus' human family from King David. The Prophet Ezekiel (1:1-14) has a vision of heavenly creatures similar to the Gospel symbols, but with four faces each: human being, lion, ox, eagle.

THE WINGED LION
WITH A BOOK

The winged lion with a book is the symbol of the Gospel of Mark, whose literary style moves as quickly as a lion. The lion was also the symbol of the Tribe of Judah, ancestors to Jesus.

THE WINGED OX
WITH A BOOK

The Winged Ox with a book is the symbol of the Gospel of Luke. The humble and hard working ox reminds us of Jesus' sacrifice. All of the Gospel symbols are based on the four "living creatures" that surround God's throne in Revelation 4.7.

THE EAGLE
WITH A BOOK

The Eagle with a book is the symbol of the Gospel of John. The soaring eagle is the monarch of the sky and reflects the "higher" theology of John's writing with its frequent depiction of the Divine nature of Jesus.

THE ROSE WINDOW

Named for the petal-like shape of its design, the rose window is the symbol of humanity's desire to seek the true meaning of life through becoming centered on God. The many paths from the circle of eternity all lead to the center image of the divine.

THE STAR OF DAVID

The Star (shield) has many meanings. The six points recall the six days of Creation and it is sometimes called the Creator's Star. The two interlocking triangles are the partnership of Divine and human. It is also the symbol of the state of Israel.

THE TABLETS
OF THE TEN COMMANDMENTS

The Mosaic Law contains 613 commandments from God to the Jewish people, but the most famous are the 10 commandments, which are usually symbolized by 2 tablets written in Hebrew.

THE 12 TRIBES

The symbols on the emblems of the Twelve Tribes of Israel vary greatly in different sources. Even the selected tribes vary, since Levi is usually not included and Manasseh and Ephraim were the sons of Joseph and sometimes substituted for him. They are based on the blessings in Genesis 49. 1-28 that Jacob, who was also called Israel, gave to his sons, who were the founders of the tribes. The only one that survived was Judah, which was to become the tribe of King David, the ancestor of Jesus.

In this group of emblems, the symbol for Manasseh is the Palm; Reuben, the sun; Benjamin, the wolf; Asher, the tree; Gad, the tent; Judah, the Lion; Joseph, the grapes; Naphtali, the doe; Simeon, the pitcher and sword; Dan, the snake; Zebulun, the boat; Issacar, the donkey.

THE LADDER

First mentioned in the Bible as a dream vision of Jacob, the ladder was a symbol of unity between God and Humanity. Jacob saw angels, God's messengers, ascending and descending steps of a ladder, which recent translations suggest were probably the steps of an ancient pyramid-like building called a ziggurat.

THE BEEHIVE

Symbol of an organized and committed Christian community, with each member working as an important member of the Body of Christ for the benefit of the whole assembly.

THE WOODPECKER

In the early days of Christianity in Central Europe, the bird became honored as the symbol of a life spent in constant prayer because of its ceaseless hammering. As the defeater of the worm, which represented evil, the woodpecker was also a Christ figure.

THE ROBIN

The robin is associated with the story of the nativity in its special diligent care for the Christ Child. At the time the robin was a small all-brown bird that spent the night watching over the child in the stable. In the middle of the night, the baby began to shiver because the coals of the stable fire were beginning to flicker out. The robin flew down close to the fire and began to flap its wings, fanning the dying coals until they began to glow again and put forth the warmth for the baby. As a reward, the robin acquired its fire-red breast to remind all of us of the joy of constant service to the Christ.

THE CARDINAL

On the night Jesus was born, legends grew about the presence of a variety of representatives from the animal world who paid homage to the Redeemer of all Creation. The Cardinal was there that night and was at the time a small, solid black bird that nobody noticed. The bird would not stop praying before the manger of the baby, no even long enough to eat. Finally an attending angel noticed the faithful bird and shined the light of heaven its way with a gentle touch turning it a bright red. The bird would not stop praying even in the presence of an angel and the next morning, when it finally raised its head, there was still a mask of its original black color to remind people to never stop praying in humility before God.

THE SERPENT

Among most cultures, ancient and modern, the serpent is a symbol of diverse and contrasting meanings. In Christianity, it is the symbol in Eden both of temptation and cleverness; in the Wilderness stories in the Book of Numbers, Moses' bronze serpent is a symbol of new life and healing.

THE WREATH

The Bible equates the wreath with the crown as a symbol of victory, joy and honor. Early Christians used it to indicate the gift of Salvation and it was often carved on gravestones. The evergreen Advent Wreath appeared in Europe shortly after World War I as a symbol of hope and preparation.

THE GREEN MAN

In early church architecture, sculptures of a human face with sprouting leaves symbolized new life and continued growth through Christ. It is also a symbol of our relationship with nature and our responsibility to preserve and protect all of Creation.

THE GRAPES

The grapes symbolize the Cup of the new Covenant, a reminder of the Sacrament of Holy Communion, also called the Eucharist or The Lord's Supper. It is one of the two Christian Sacraments instituted by Jesus of Nazareth.

THE CORAL

Since it was believed to be a "tree" that could live forever, even under water, coral came to be the symbol for the Garden of Eden's Tree of Life. In the 16th century, the "coral of life" was thought to be a cure for almost anything including stopping blood flow from a wound, turning madness into wisdom and blocking magical curses.

THE ROOSTER

A symbol of Simon Peter's denial of Jesus. He was told that before a rooster crowed twice, he would have denied knowing Jesus three times.

THE DRAGON

As in many cultures, the dragon is the Christian symbol of massive destruction, both of our physical environment and of our own spirits through evil thoughts. In the Book of the Revelation, the rampaging dragon is the symbol of God's worst enemy.

THE BEE

An early symbol of the wisdom of God. The wise Prophet Deborah's name meant bee in Hebrew. The bee also symbolized the Holy Spirit because of its tireless work and Christ because its honey represented gentleness and compassion; its stinger the symbol of judgment.

Dove With Olive Branch

One of the most famous symbols of peace on earth is the dove carrying an olive branch. Appearing in the Book of Genesis at the end of the flood story, the dove follows the raven as a scout to bring back evidence of dry land so that the residents of the ark could safely disembark. When the raven did not return, Noah sent the dove who did return carrying an olive branch as an indication the earth was in the process of renewal. After the turmoil of the flood, there was once again peace on earth. The dove is also a frequent symbol for the Holy Spirit.

Fleur De Lis

A popular flower symbol of Mary of Nazareth; the stylized lily or iris with its humble downward turned petals remind us of Mary's acceptance of God's will. The angel Gabriel is often pictured holding a stalk of lilies.

THE ROSEMARY

There are several old Christmas legends about the rosemary plant that associate it with Mary. In Spain the story goes, the shrub served as a shelter for Mary and the Holy Family as they made their flight to Egypt. The legends continue, relating that Mary, after a long and dusty journey stopped by the rosemary bush to spread out and dry her laundry on top of the soft leaves as the family made the return journey from Bethlehem. When her traditionally blue garment was removed from the plant, it had blossomed with tiny blue flowers and acquired its characteristic pleasant fragrance.

THE FIVE POINTED STAR

The symbol of a five pointed star is very often seen on the flags of the world as well as many national seals and emblems. Its shape represents the head, outstretched arms and firmly planted legs of a divine being who is standing guard over a particular people or country. The five pointed star was also a powerful divine protection symbol in Heraldry, identified as a mullet.

THE LABYRINTH

An ancient design that resembles a maze, but with only one path in and out. In early Christian churches, the labyrinth on the floor symbolized the many paths and detours humankind takes on the way to a spiritual Jerusalem, represented as the middle of the curving path.

I.N.R.I.

The initials I.N.R.I. stand for the mocking words of the Latin sign posted above Jesus on the cross: Jesus Nazarenus Rex Judaeorum. In Roman type, the "J" was written as an English "I". It means Jesus of Nazareth, King of the Jews.

SYMBOLS OF THE SEASONS

ADVENT

The Season of Advent is when we look forward to the imminent arrival of the Christ into the world. It is a time of anticipation and excitement, but also a time of profound consideration and penitence as we pause and reorient ourselves to the true meaning of the presence of Christ in our lives.

How beautiful upon the mountain are the feet of the messenger who announces peace, who brings good news, who announces salvation. Isaiah 52.7

The word advent originates in the Latin word advenio, meaning come towards. The closer the Nativity of Christ comes toward us, the more we "overflow with hope" (Romans 15.4). Like Elizabeth in the Gospel of Luke, we feel the "child with us" kicking at the nearness of Christ.

SYMBOLS OF THE SEASON

Advent Candles:
Each candle in the circumference of the wreath represents a gift of the Holy Spirit; hope, peace, joy (the pink candle) and love. The white center candle is the Christ Candle, which is lit on Christmas day. The weekly candle lighting ritual symbolizes the steady keeping of the faith.

Herald Angel:
Reminders of the angels who told the shepherds of Bethlehem to "Fear not," angels with their right hands raised in greeting are symbols of the coming Nativity.

Dove of Peace:
The dove carrying an olive branch from the story of the Great Flood is a symbol of the bringer of peace on earth and the anticipation of a new way of life.

CHRISTMASTIDE

The short Season of Christmastide is 12 Days long and lasts between Christmas Day (December 25) and the Feast of the Epiphany (January 6). Epiphany Eve (January 5) is known as Twelfth Night, ending the 12 Days of Christmas. Christmas is the most celebrated time of the Christian year and rich in traditions of gift giving, decorating and music making, demonstrating that our waiting is over, our joy is complete; God in Christ is incarnate among us.

For the grace of God has appeared, bringing salvation to all. Titus 2.11

The word Christmas refers to the worship service or mass that celebrates the birth of Christ. In French the season is called Noel, meaning the Good News and in many other languages, such as Natale in Italian, the name of the season celebrates the birth.

SYMBOLS OF THE SEASON

The Christmas Tree:
Reminders of the "tongues of fire" symbolizing the all-consuming power of the Holy Spirit.

The Poinsettia:
Another Holy Spirit symbol, the white meaning purity and a remembrance of the "Spirit descending on Jesus like a dove as he emerged from the waters of Baptism.

The Manger:
The Feast of the First Fruits was a Jewish springtime harvest observance. In Christian terms it came to mean the tasting of the first fruits of the Realm of God.

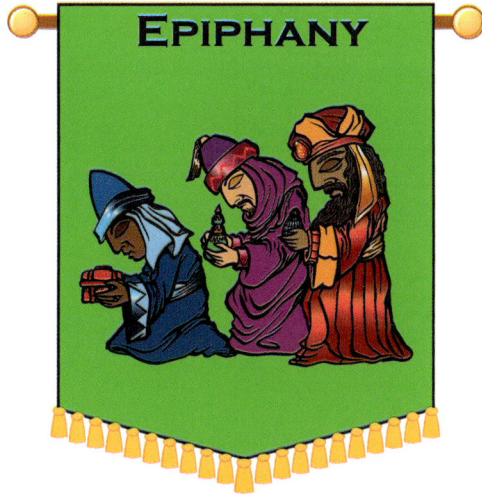

EPIPHANY

The Season of Epiphany remembers the adoration of the Magi, the wise ones from the east who recognized the universal coming of the Christ to Jew and Gentile alike. The Greek word epipheneia means showing or manifestation. The season also recalls the first public appearances of the adult Jesus, who announces the Dominion of God to all people.

I am the light of the world. The one who follows me will not walk in darkness, but will have the light of life. John 8.12

The Gospel of Matthew is the only source of information about the mysterious Magi. All else is speculation. Since they were guided by the star, they could have been astrologers. The great value of their gifts has contributed to the legend that they could also have been kings. Tradition has named them Melchior, Caspar and Balthazzar.

SYMBOLS OF THE SEASON

The Three Gifts:

The gold represents the royalty of Christ, both through God the Creator and the line of King David. Frankincense is a fragrant resin burned to symbolize Christ's Divine Presence and also his role as High Priest. Myrrh, an ointment that was used for anointing bodies at burial foretells Christ's death. Matthew tells us about the three gifts, but not the number of the magi themselves.

The Star of Bethlehem:
The light in the sky that guided the Magi reminds us that Jesus is the Light of the World.

The Three Ships:
Traditionally, when the Magi departed the region "by another way" in order to avoid further contact with King Herod, they traveled by ships.

LENT

The Season of Lent is the most important time of penitence, reflection and prayer in the Christian calendar. It is a period of self-examination, meditation and alms-giving. Lent lasts for forty days in remembrance of the forty days Jesus spent in his time of trial in the wilderness. The word lent comes from the Old English word lengten, or lengthen, referring to the lengthening of days in the spring.

Seek the LORD and live. Amos 5.6

Lent originated in the forth century as a time of preparation for people who were to be baptized on Easter. It has since become a season when we concentrate on the strengthening our spirits through fasting from food or giving up certain luxuries in favor of taking something on, such as being active in the world for the benefit of others, especially for the poor. It is also a time of study of the scriptures and spiritual teachings, both as individuals and in community.

SYMBOLS OF THE SEASON

Palm Leaves:
The palm leaves were waved by the crowd on Palm Sunday in greeting the triumphal entry of Jesus into Jerusalem.

Cup & Loaf:
The cup and loaf remind us of the institution of the sacrament of the Eucharist, or Holy Communion, on Maundy Thursday of Holy Week.

The Crown of Thorns:
The Crown of Thorns was worn by Jesus in his Passion as he was mocked on his way to the cross.

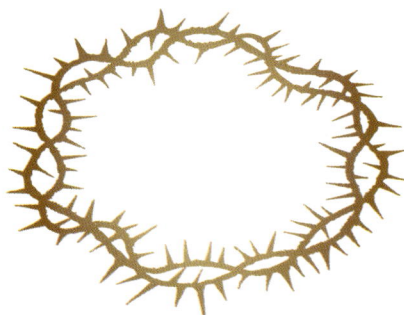

The Jerusalem Cross:
The Jerusalem Cross is a representation of the five wounds of Christ in his hands, feet and side.

EASTERTIDE

Eastertide lasts for 50 days, from Resurrection (Easter) Sunday until the Day of Pentecost. It is the season of the church year when we most remember and celebrate the presence of the risen Christ among us and the power of God to bring new life

Mary Magdalene went and announced to the disciples, 'I have seen the Lord' John 20.18

Eastertide is a good time of the year to think about organization and delegation as we remember Christ's charge to Peter to "feed my lambs" and tend my sheep."

SYMBOLS OF THE SEASON

The Empty Tomb:

The main symbol during Eastertide of the victory of life over death. All four Gospels tell of the empty tomb being discovered early in the morning by Mary Magdalene who, in some of the stories, was accompanied by several other women.

The Egg:

A symbol of birth in many religions. The early Christians adopted it as a reminder of Christ emerging from the tomb. (New life from a lifeless object.) Colorful painted eggs help us celebrate the joy of the Season.

The Paschal Candle:

The symbol of Christ's light and presence in the midst of the people. The tall candle decorated with a variety of other Christian symbols is also known as the Easter candle or the Christ candle. "Paschal" comes from the Hebrew word pesach, which means Passover

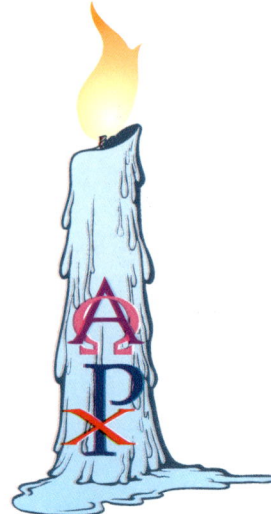

PENTECOST

The Season of Pentecost celebrates the descent of the Holy Spirit upon the disciples ten days after the Ascension of Jesus. It is the season when we seek guidance through the Spirit in putting our faith into practice by working out the social consequences of Christ's teachings. "Pentecost" is Greek for "the fiftieth day" and is historically related to the Jewish harvest festival of Shavuot, fifty days after the Passover Feast.

And suddenly a sound came from above like the rush of a mighty wind, and filled all the house where they were sitting. And there appeared to them tongues as of fire resting on each of them.
Acts 2.2-3

Because this marks the time the disciples were empowered to go out into the streets with the understanding and the strength to speak the Good News of Christ, Pentecost is called the "birthday of the church."

Symbols of the Season

The Flames:
Reminders of the "tongues of fire" symbolizing the all-consuming power of the Holy Spirit.

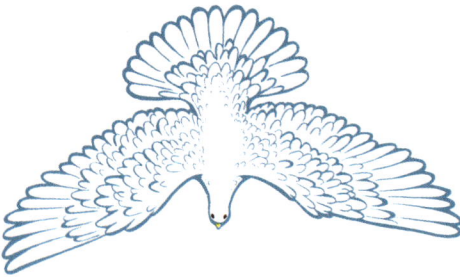

The Descending Dove:
Another Holy Spirit symbol, the white meaning purity and a remembrance of the "Spirit descending on Jesus like a dove as he emerged from the waters of Baptism.

The First Fruits:
The Feast of the First Fruits was a Jewish springtime harvest observance. In Christian terms it came to mean the tasting of the first fruits of the Realm of God.

DOMINIONTIDE

The Season of Dominiontide (also called Kingdomtide or Kindomtide) emphasizes the principles of the Dominion of God on earth and our social responsibility to be witnesses for justice as members of that Dominion. It is a time we remember God's unconditional inclusion and seek ways to share that good news with all the nations and peoples of the world.

There is no longer Jew or Greek, there is no longer slave or free, there is no longer male and female, for all of you are one in Christ Jesus. Galatians 3.28

Dominiontide originated as Kingdomtide, a Methodist Episcopal Church season, adopted in 1939, which began on the last Sunday of August and continued until Advent. (Other traditions call the months between the Seasons of Pentecost and Advent Ordinary Time.)

SYMBOLS OF THE SEASON

The Cross Triumphant:
Also known as the Cross of Victory; symbol of the announcement of the Good News of Christ throughout all the earth.

Burning Torch:
A symbol of witness. (Let your light shine before others, so that they might see your good works and give glory to your Creator in heaven. Matthew 5.16)

The Triangle:
Symbol of the Dominion of God in the unity of the Trinity (Creator, Christ and Holy Spirit.)

THE LITURGICAL COLORS

BLUE

As a liturgical color, blue is the color of heaven; of the divine. It represents purity, truth and fidelity. It is also the color of the fantastic and the unknowable mysteries of God. In icon art, blue clothing in being symbolic of divinity, contrasts to the red clothing of humankind; red symbolizing the flowing blood of life.

GREEN

As a liturgical color, green reminds us of the evergreen, always patiently growing in strength and stature. It can also signify new birth as the color of the renewal of life in springtime. In the middle ages, artists sometimes painted the Cross of Christ green as a sign of renewal and hope; a replacement for Eden's original "Tree of Life."

VIOLET

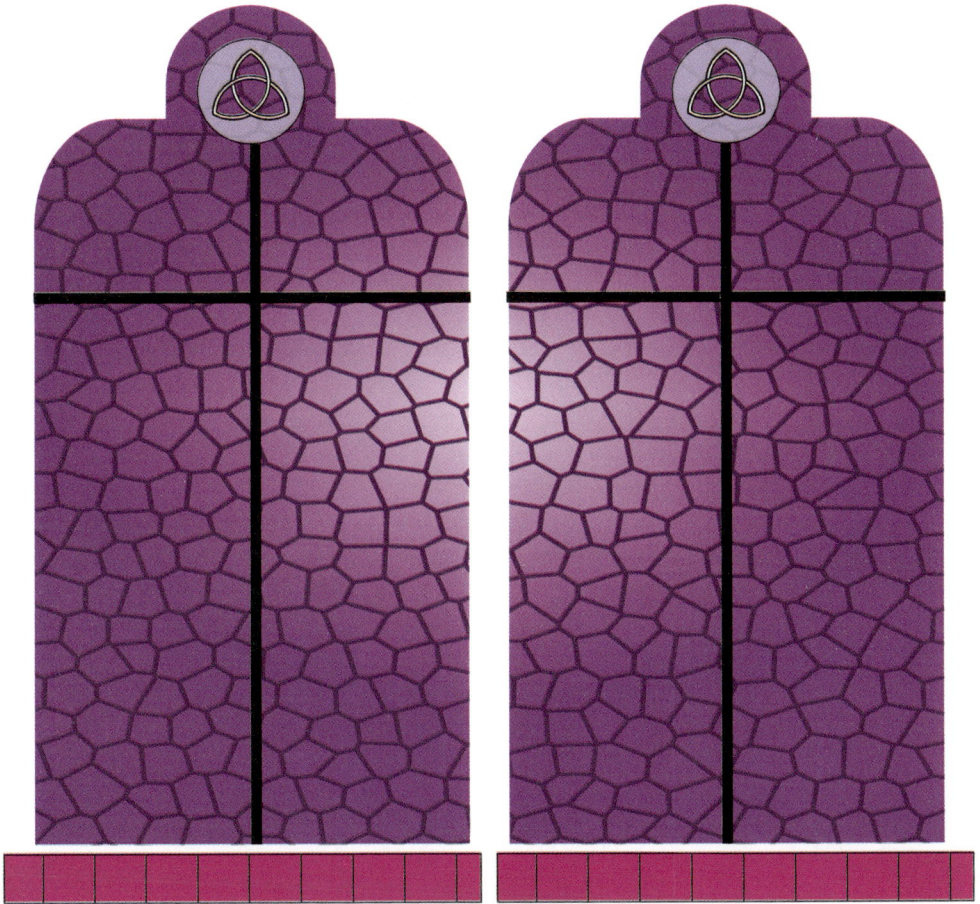

Violet, or purple, as a liturgical color, symbolizes the partnership or cooperation between God and humankind. It is the symbol of balance in meditation. As a mixture of blue (the divine color) and red (the human color) violet is the complete union of God and humanity through Christ's life and death.

WHITE

White, as a liturgical color, is the presence of purity, perfection and light. In the light spectrum, it is the combination of all colors making it the hue of inclusion and the symbol of joy at all major church feast days. When Jesus was transfigured, even his clothing was described as glowing "white as snow."

BLACK

The opposite of white, in liturgical colors, black can be symbolic of the complete absence of light. Since, in paint pigments, it is the presence of all colors, black is also a symbol of deep thought, contemplation and wisdom. Black clothing is often worn as a sign of mourning and on holy occasions remembering Christ's passion.

RED

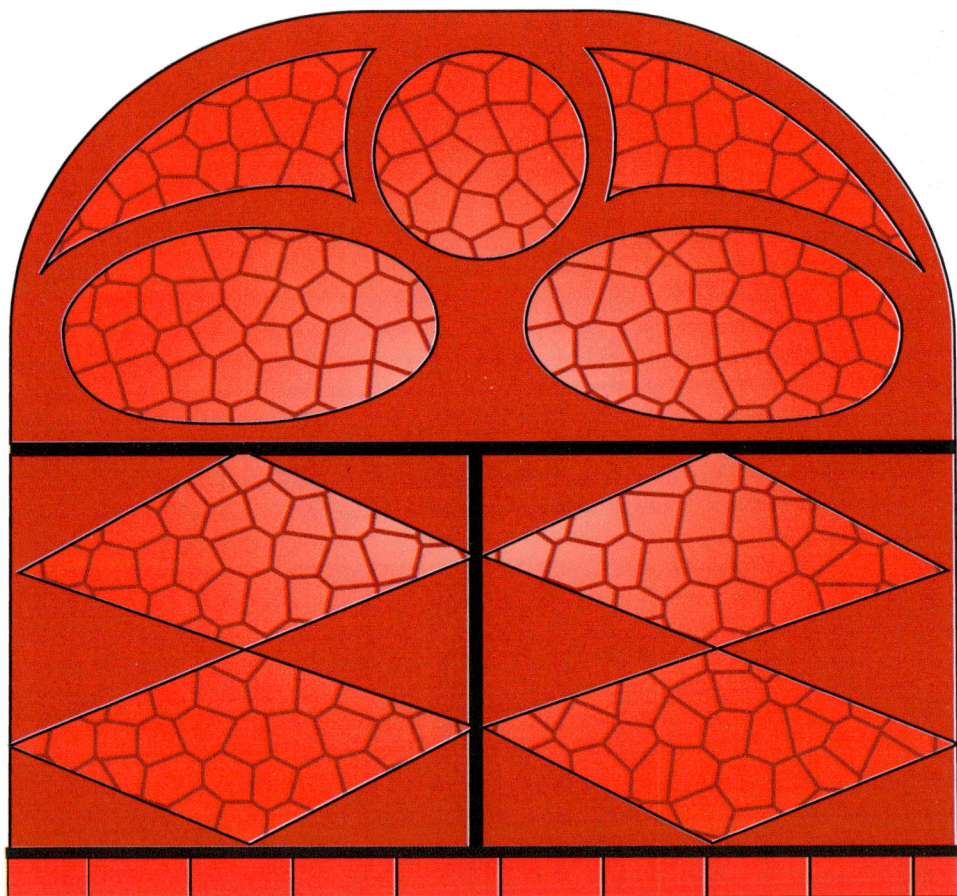

Red has several meanings as a liturgical color. It is the color of blood and a reminder of both the vital flow of life and the deaths of martyrs of the church. Red is both the color of humanity and of fire, which is often the symbol of the presence of God, as in the flames of Moses' burning bush, the Pillar of Fire and Pentecost's tongues of fire.

About the authors / Illustrators

Dan Peeler

Charlie Rose

Dan Peeler and Charlie Rose have worked together in the film and TV business as animators, artists, writers and puppeteers since 1981.

Combining their talent, Rose and Peeler formed their Dallas, Texas-based family entertainment company, Peeler-Rose Productions in 1989. Highlights of their career include animated segments for *Sesame Street* and *The Electric Company,* re-designing the Chuck E. Cheese brand characters and logos, two animated specials for the Disney Channel, *Bugs Bunny In CartoonLand* storybook, and design and production of the live-action children's program for PBS and The Learning Channel, *Bobby Goldsboro's Swamp Critters of Lost Lagoon.*

In recent years, the team has written and illustrated over 200 childrens educational stories, PowerPoint lessons, books and classroom curriculum, centered on progressive Christian themes.

They are currently Artists-In-Residence at the Old Jail Art Center in Albany, Texas.

23912776R00059

Made in the USA
Lexington, KY
28 June 2013